THE
FACTS ON
THE
MORMON
CHURCH

JOHN ANKERBERG
& JOHN WELDON

HARVEST HOUSE™ PUBLISHERS

EUGENE, OREGON

Cover by Terry Dugan Design, Minneapolis, Minnesota

The Facts On Series
by John Ankerberg and John Weldon

The Facts on Halloween

The Facts on Homosexuality

The Facts on Islam

The Facts on Jehovah's Witnesses

The Facts on the King James Only Debate

The Facts on the Masonic Lodge

The Facts on the Mormon Church

The Facts on Roman Catholicism

THE FACTS ON THE MORMON CHURCH
Copyright © 1991 by The Ankerberg Theological Research Institute
Published by Harvest House Publishers
Eugene, Oregon 97402
www.harvesthousepublishers.com

Library of Congress Cataloging-in-Publication Data
Ankerberg, John, 1945–
  The facts on the Mormon Church / John Ankerberg and John Weldon.
    p. cm. —(Facts on series)
Originally published: Eugene, Or. : Harvest House, ©1991, in series: Ankerberg, John, 1945– Anker series. Includes bibliographical references.
  ISBN-13: 978-0-7369-1114-6 (pbk.)
  ISBN-10: 0-7369-1114-6 (pbk.)
  1. Mormon Church—Controversial literature—Miscellanea. 2. Mormon Church—Doctrines—Miscellanea. I. Weldon, John. II. Title.
BX8645 .A683 2003
289.3—dc21
                                                          2002010766

Printed in the United States of America
    06 07 08 09 10 11 / VP-CF / 11 10 9 8 7 6

CONTENTS

Section I
Introduction to Mormonism

Section II
Is Mormon Teaching the Same as Biblical and Christian Teaching?

Section III
Mormonism—A Critical Evaluation

Section IV
Mormonism and the Occult: Should Mormonism
Be Considered an Occult Religion?

SECTION I

Introduction to Mormonism

1

What is Mormonism, and why is it important?

Mormonism is a religion founded upon the teachings of Joseph Smith (1805–1844). Although some 100 Mormon sects have existed historically (many of which are polygamous), the two largest divisions are the Church of Jesus Christ of Latter-day Saints (headquartered in Salt Lake City, Utah) and the Community of Christ, formerly the Reorganized Church of Latter-day Saints (headquartered in Independence, Missouri).

The subject of Mormonism is important because of the Church's influence, power, and evangelistic operations. For example, it maintains over 60,000 missionaries who actively engage in proselytizing activities throughout the world.[1] Further, boasting a membership of 12 million worldwide, Mormonism is also the fourth largest religion in the U.S. (more than 6 million adherents). Indeed, *The New Mormon Challenge*, a scholarly critique of recent LDS apologetics, extrapolates current growth rates to 580 million by the end of this century. Although the LDS Church doesn't release financial records, the leadership granted *Time* magazine unusual cooperation. In the August 4, 1997 issue, the LDS assets were valued at a minimum of $30 billion. The same article estimated an annual gross income of $5.9 billion.

No one can doubt the power and influence of Mormonism. [2, 3]

2

How did Mormonism originate, and how important are supernatural revelations to the founding and sustaining of the Mormon Church?

Like most other religions, Mormonism claims divine inspiration as its source. Mormons argue that their religion was divinely instituted in 1820 when

God the Father and Jesus Christ allegedly appeared to Joseph Smith in a dramatic vision. "Jesus" told Smith that Christianity was in complete apostasy and that he (Smith) would be guided into the truth, for the reestablishment of true Christian faith.

This crucial "first vision" of Joseph Smith is the official account of Mormon beginnings. Although it allegedly establishes the Church's divine origin, there are at least six contradictory versions of this key event.[4] (See Question 15.) The Church's current official and least likely version follows:

Joseph Smith claimed that in his fifteenth year, while living in Manchester, New York, a religious revival of significant proportions took place "and great multitudes united themselves to the different religious parties."[5] Smith claimed that the strife among these parties was so great as to confuse a person as to which one was correct in its teachings—Presbyterians, Baptists, Methodist, or some other denomination. Because of this alleged strife, Smith determined to privately seek God's counsel as to which of the various denominations he should join.

One day while reading James 1:5 (which refers to asking God for wisdom), Smith was greatly moved. In Smith's own words:

> Never did any passage of scripture come home with more power to the heart of man than this did at this time to mine....[Smith then retired to a secluded place in the woods to seek God's counsel]....I kneeled down and began to offer up the desires of my heart to God. I had scarcely done so, when immediately I was seized upon by some power which entirely overcame me, and had such an astonishing influence over me as to bind my tongue so that I could not speak. Thick darkness gathered around me, and it seemed to me for a time as if I were doomed to sudden destruction.
>
> But, exerting all my powers to call upon God to deliver me out of the power of this enemy which had seized upon me...just at this moment of great alarm, I saw a pillar of light exactly over my head above the brightness of the sun, which descended gradually until it fell upon me. It no sooner appeared when I found myself delivered from the enemy which held me bound.

> When the light rested upon me, I saw two Personages whose brightness and glory defy all description standing above me in the air. One of them spake unto me, calling me by name, and said, pointing to the other—*"This is My Beloved Son. Hear Him!"*
>
> My object in going to inquire of the Lord was to know which of all the [religious] sects was right, that I might know which to join. No sooner, therefore, did I get possession of myself, so as to be able to speak, than I asked the Personages who stood above me in the light, which of all the sects was right—and which I should join.
>
> I was answered that I must join none of them, for they were all wrong, and the Personage who addressed me [presumably Jesus Christ] said that all their creeds were an abomination in his sight: that those professors were all corrupt; that: "they draw near to me with their lips, but their hearts are far from me, they teach for doctrines the commandments of men, having a form of godliness, but they deny the power thereof." He again forbade me to join with any of them: and many other things did he say....[6]

Although Smith's claims were considered impossible by the Christian community, Joseph remained true to his vision. His "mind [was satisfied] so far as the sectarian [Christian] world was concerned....It was not my duty to join with any of them, but to continue as I was until further directed."[7]

Unfortunately, if Joseph Smith had truly believed in the authority of the Bible and had really studied it, he could have determined for himself that the various Christian denominations were *not* "all corrupt" and that the vision was, therefore, a false one.[8] Nor, apparently, was he aware of the characteristic methods of spiritistic imposture.[9]

But Smith was convinced that he had been called of God and, although in the next three years he confesses he "frequently fell into many foolish errors" (cf. James 1:20-22,26), he waited patiently for the next revelation.[10]

On September 21, 1823, an "angel" appeared to Smith telling him of the location of certain "gold plates." It was from the writings on these gold plates that eventually the Mormon scripture known as the Book of Mormon was allegedly "translated." These plates supposedly contained the historical records of a tribe of Jewish people known as the "Nephites" concerning their supposed early migration to the Americas.[11]

Smith had many more claimed angelic revelations. Just as the LDS Church ostensibly began through supernatural revelation, it was also sustained by this process. For example, from 1831 to 1844, Smith allegedly "received 135 direct revelations from God," helping the new movement to grow and solidify itself.[12] Smith believed that he received revelations from God, Jesus, and many spirits of the dead, such as Peter, James, John the Baptist, and others.[13] (See Questions 21-23. Many of these revelations are printed in *Doctrine and Covenants*, the second and doctrinally most important volume of Mormon scriptures.)[14]

3

How can we know if these revelations were from God or whether they originated from some other source?

That Joseph Smith or anyone else claims to have divine visions does not automatically prove the visions are from God; people may invent stories of divine visions for unknown reasons or they may even be the recipient of mental delusions. Even if Joseph Smith was the recipient of *genuine* supernatural manifestations, how does anyone know they were not clever counterfeits by deceiving spirits who were lying when they claimed to be angels and saints?[15]

The issue of Mormon revelations is finally reduced to one simple test. If Joseph Smith's revelations deny, contradict, and oppose the Bible, then whatever their source, they cannot possibly have originated in God. And if they did not originate in God, they have no divine authority and should not be heeded.

Most of this book will be devoted to supplying documentation that Mormon revelations and the doctrine derived from them cannot be considered divine. If you are a Mormon, we ask you to carefully weigh the arguments presented. Every conscientious religious person has a responsibility to be certain that what he or she claims to be from God really is from Him (1 Thessalonians 5:21; 1 John 4:1).[16]

4

Does Mormonism claim to be the only true church on earth?

Mormonism does not claim to be one part of the Christian religion, such as a Christian denomination. Rather, it claims to comprise the only true Christian religion on earth. This is in harmony with the "first vision" of Joseph Smith, where Jesus supposedly condemned all Christian religions as corrupt abominations. *Doctrine and Covenants* emphasizes that Mormonism is "the only true and living church upon the face of the whole earth."[17]

Indeed, from their earliest days, Mormons have claimed they were the only people of God on earth. In 1854, leading Mormon Orson Pratt argued, "All other churches are entirely destitute of all authority from God."[18] A leading doctrinal theologian of the modern Mormon Church, the late Bruce McConkie, asserted that "Mormons…have the only pure and perfect Christianity now on earth."[19] He also taught, "All other systems of religion are false."[20] The Mormon Sunday school text, *The Master's Church, Course A,* informs children, "We cannot accept that any other church can lead its members to salvation.…"[21]

5

Is Mormonism a Christian religion?

Many people accept the Mormon faith as genuinely Christian. But when Christians view Mormons as believers, they have failed to understand Mormonism correctly. They have accepted Mormon claims without determining whether those claims are true.[22, 23, 24]

Virtually all knowledgeable Christian authorities recognize that not only is Mormonism not Christian, it is really anti-Christian. The late Dr. Anthony Hoekema declared in his book *The Four Major Cults:* "We must at this point assert, in the strongest possible terms, that Mormonism does not deserve to be called a Christian religion. It is basically anti-Christian and anti-biblical."[25] Gordon Fraser, the author of four books on Mormonism, explained, "We object to Mormon missionaries posing as Christians, and our objections are based on the differences between what they are taught by their [Mormon] General Authorities and what the Bible teaches."[26] One of the leading modern authorities on the cults, the late Dr. Walter Martin, correctly asserted, "In no uncertain terms, the Bible condemns the teachings of the Mormon Church."[27] Former Mormons and leading experts on Mormonism, Jerald and Sandra Tanner, also correctly affirm, "The Mormon Church is certainly not built on the teachings of the Bible."[28]

If the teachings of Mormonism are biblical, then they deserve to be called Christian. But if Mormon teachings deny and oppose biblical teaching, then it is wrong for anyone to consider Mormonism a Christian religion. In our next question, we will briefly illustrate how Mormon teachings oppose biblical teachings. We will do this by showing that when the Mormon Church uses a Christian term, it typically rejects the biblical definition of that term and substitutes a false, non-Christian definition in its place.

6

Does the Mormon Church give biblical words an entirely false meaning?

In order to illustrate that Mormon teachings are not biblical, we have provided a selected list of key biblical/Christian words and the false definitions the

Mormon Church gives to them. This redefinition of words underscores the problem we face when discussing religious issues with Mormons. Unless Christians pursue the meaning of such words, and unless Mormons are frank in giving them their true Mormon definition, Christians and the public in general will continue to be confused over the religious status of Mormonism.

In any discussion with a Mormon, the following redefinition of terms must be kept in mind. Although Mormons themselves may not be aware of some of the definitions cited below, they represent true Mormon teaching as proven by an evaluation of standard Mormon theological works.[29] (Section II provides illustrations.)

Christianity: sectarianism; a false and damnable apostate religion.

God: "Elohim"; one of innumerable self-progressing bodily deities; formerly a man, a finite creature. In early Mormon theology, Adam (of the Garden of Eden) was considered by many Mormons as the true earth deity.[30]

Jesus Christ: a self-progressing deity ("Jehovah" of the Old Testament) and the first spirit child of "Elohim" and his wife.

Holy Ghost: a man with a spiritual body of matter.

Trinity: tritheistic; coordinated under general Mormon polytheism; thus the Father, Son, and Holy Ghost are separate deities.

The Gospel: Mormon salvation by works leading to exaltation or godhood.

Born-again: water baptism into Mormonism.

Immortality: salvation by grace (the universal resurrection of all men).

Atonement: the provision God has supplied for people to earn their own salvation "by obedience to the laws and ordinances of the Gospel" (*Articles of Faith*, 3).

The Fall: a spiritual step upward; a blessing permitting the production of physical bodies for preexistent spirits to inhabit and thus have the possibility of attaining their own "exaltation" or godhood.

True salvation/eternal life/redemption: exaltation to godhood in the highest part of the celestial kingdom based upon individual good works and personal merit; exaltation incorporates ruling a new world and sexual procreation in order to produce spirit children who will eventually be embodied and inhabit that world, each then having the opportunity to be exalted or deified.

Death: generally a step upward; death represents the possibility of a form of salvation (if not exaltation) for those who have never heard of Mormonism.

Heaven: three "kingdoms of glory" comprising various spiritual gradations.

Hell: generally purgatorial; possibly eternal for a very few (primarily apostate Mormons).

Virgin birth: the birth of Christ through a physical sex act between God the Father (the Mormon earth god "Elohim") and Mary (hence, *not* a virgin birth).

Man: a preexistent spirit with the potential to earn godhood by obedience to Mormon dictates.

Creation: the reorganization of eternal matter.

The Scriptures: the Book of Mormon, *Doctrine and Covenants*, *The Pearl of Great Price*, and the Bible "as far as it is translated correctly" (*Articles of Faith*, 8).

The Bible: an erring and often unreliable inspired record, properly interpreted only by Mormons and only in light of Mormon theology.

For 2,000 years the Christian church has expressed general agreement on the meanings of these terms. Yet the Mormon definitions and descriptions of them are anything but Christian. Why has the Mormon Church supplied false definitions to common Christian terms? Because it has not relied upon the Bible alone to formulate its views. It has depended upon revelations from the spirit world (see Section IV), and these revelations have forced a redefinition of terms. Once these revelations had become the Church's standard scriptures, the doctrinal teachings of the Mormon Church were predetermined.

This is why Mormonism cannot be considered Christian—its new revelations deny the true meaning of biblical terms and offer non-Christian teachings in their place.

In our next section, we will contrast specific Mormon and Christian doctrines so readers can easily see the fundamental irreconcilability of Mormonism with Christianity.

SECTION II

Is Mormon Teaching
the Same as Biblical
and Christian
Teaching?

7

How do Mormon teachings differ from Christian teachings?

Because Mormon theology is not Christian, it is easy to compare the beliefs of Mormonism with the beliefs of Christianity. As an introduction to this section, we offer the following chart contrasting basic Mormon and Christian teachings.

Mormonism	Christianity
Bible	*Bible*
Unreliable	Reliable
Incomplete as it is	Complete as it is
Adds new revelations to God's Word	Rejects new revelations
Unbiblical theological presuppositions utilized in interpretation	Accepted hermeneutical rules utilized in interpretation
God	*God*
Tritheism/polytheistic	Trinity/monotheistic
Physical (evolved man)	Spirit
Finite	Infinite
Morally questionable	Holy
Organizer of eternal matter	Creator of matter from nothing
Sexual polygamist	Asexual
Jesus	*Jesus*
A god	God
Created	Eternal
Earned salvation (exaltation to godhood)	As eternal God neither salvation nor exaltation required

(continued)

Not virgin born	Virgin born
Polygamist*	Unmarried
Salvation	**Salvation**
By works	By grace
Denies biblical atonement	Affirms atonement
Possible after death	Impossible after death
Death	**Death**
"Purgatorial"; three celestial kingdoms; almost universalistic	Eternal heaven or hell; no purgatory; not universalistic

Maintaining that Mormonism and Christianity teach the same thing is logically, historically, and doctrinally an indefensible position. We will now document the LDS attitude toward Christianity and some of the key doctrines of Mormonism and show why they are not biblical.

8

How does Mormonism view the Christian religion?

The Mormon Church teaches that shortly after the time of the disciples, the Christian church apostatized and was not restored until Joseph Smith's "first vision" in 1820. (See Question 14.) Therefore, Mormonism considers Christianity an enemy because it teaches "false" doctrines. Because Mormonism holds that Christian doctrines lead men astray spiritually, the Mormon Church views Christians as deceived people.

Second president Brigham Young taught that Christians were unbelievers; they may falsely claim to believe in Christ, but the truth is "not one of them

---

* Primarily, but not exclusively, an early Mormon teaching.

really believes in Him."[31] Further, Joseph Smith emphasized that Christian pastors "are of their father, the devil" and they and all who follow them "without one exception [will] receive their portion with the devil and his angels."[32] Smith avowed they will "all be damned together."[33-36]

In *Journal of Discourses*, a 27-volume set of authoritative speeches by early Mormon presidents and leaders, we find the following. Brigham Young taught that concerning true theology, "a more ignorant people never lived than the present so-called Christian world."[37] He also believed that Christians were "heathens as to their knowledge of the salvation of God."[38] John Taylor, the third president of the Church, believed that Christianity was a "perfect pack of nonsense…as corrupt as hell" and an invention of the devil.[39] He taught that Mormons were "the saviors of the world" and the entire Christian world knew nothing about God—that as far as "the things of God are concerned, they are the veriest fools…."[40]

The apostle Orson Pratt, another leader in the early Church, declared, "The whole of Christendom is as destitute of Bible Christianity as the idolatrous pagans."[41] In his 1854 article "Repentance," he asked, "How long will the heavens suffer such wickedness to go unpunished?"[42] According to Pratt:

> [Christians] will, every soul of them, unless they repent of these false doctrines, be cast down to hell.…Every one of you will, most assuredly, be damned.[43]

The tenth president of the Mormon Church, Joseph Fielding Smith, claimed that the supposed apostasy of Christianity had caused it to become a pagan "abomination."[44]

Nor has modern Mormonism changed its mind. Leading Mormon theologian Bruce McConkie referred to Christian churches as "churches of the devil."[45, 46, 47]

In another book, McConkie alleged that Christians are enemies of God, because God's plan of salvation "has been changed and perverted by an apostate Christendom."[48] Modern Christians are not only ignorant of God's true purposes,[49] their doctrines are "the doctrines of devils,"[50] and the Christian church is part of the "great and abominable church" of the devil preparing men "to be damned."[51]

All this is proof that the Mormon Church views the Christian faith as its enemy and individual Christians as spiritually deceived people.[52]

9

What does Mormonism teach about God?

Mormons emphasize that they believe in the biblical God, and they "believe in the Holy Trinity."[53] But this claim is demonstrably false. We compare and contrast the Mormon concept of deity with the Christian concept in the following chart.

The Mormon God	The Biblical God
Many (polytheistic)	One (monotheistic)
Evolving (changing)	Immutable (unchanging)
Material (physical)	Immaterial (spirit)
Sexual	Asexual
Polygamist	Celibate
Morally imperfect (e.g., requiring salvation)	Eternally holy

Let us briefly examine these Mormon views of deity in turn. First, the Mormon Church accepts and teaches what is known as *polytheism*, a belief in many gods.* This is in contrast to historic, orthodox Christian teaching that asserts there is only one God.

---

* Technically, Mormon belief is henotheistic—a polytheistic system stressing one central deity ("Elohim," the primary god of this earth).

Mormons will often claim they believe in only one God and that they are not polytheists, but such claims are false.

In his own words, Joseph Smith, the founder of Mormonism, emphasized, "I wish to declare I have always and in all congregations where I have preached on the subject of deity, it has [been on] the plurality of Gods."[54] In *Mormon Doctrine*, McConkie declares, "There are three Gods—the Father, Son and Holy Ghost."[55] McConkie further confesses,

> …to us speaking in the proper finite sense, these three are the only Gods we worship. But, in addition, there is an infinite number of holy personages, drawn from worlds without number, who have passed on to exaltation and are thus Gods….This doctrine of plurality of Gods is so comprehensive and glorious that it reaches out and embraces every exalted personage. Those who attain exaltation are Gods.[56]

In other words, not only are there three principal gods for this earth, and not only are there an infinite number of gods throughout infinite worlds, but every Mormon who is "exalted" will himself become a god—in the fullest sense of that term.[57]

But this is clearly not the teaching of the Bible. The God of the Bible says, "Before Me there was no God formed, and there will be none after Me" (Isaiah 43:10). He also says, "I am the first and I am the last, and there is no God besides Me….Is there any God besides Me….I know of none" (Isaiah 44:6,8). Finally, God declares, "I am the Lord, and there is no other; besides Me there is no God….There is none except Me" (Isaiah 45:5,21). What could be clearer?

When Mormonism teaches there are many gods—indeed an infinite number of them—it denies what God Himself teaches in His Word.

Further, Mormonism teaches that each god is evolving. Even though God Himself has said, "I, the Lord, do not change" (Malachi 3:6; cf. James 1:17; Numbers 23:19), Mormonism teaches that God was once a man, having been created by another god. But by self-perfection, this man finally evolved into absolute godhood. McConkie confesses Mormon belief when he teaches, "God is a Holy Man."[58] Joseph Smith likewise taught that "God Himself, the Father of us all…was once a man like us."[59] In his own words, Joseph Smith made his beliefs plain:

> God Himself was once as we are now, and is an exalted man and sits enthroned in yonder heavens! That is the great secret….If you were to see him today, you would see him like a man in form….I am going to tell you how God came to be God. We have imagined and supposed that God was God from all eternity. I will refute that idea, and take away the veil, so that you may see….He was once a man like us….Here, then, is eternal life—to know the only wise and true God; and you have got to learn how to be Gods yourselves.[60, 61]

Nevertheless, the Bible is clear that God is an unchanging, infinite being existing from all eternity—not a finite man who somehow evolved into godhood (Job 9:32; Numbers 23:19). "For I am God, and not man—the Holy One among you" (Hosea 11:9 NIV).

Although the Bible affirms that "God is spirit" (John 4:24), the Mormon Church denies what the Bible teaches and tells its members that God is not spirit, but rather a physical being. Joseph Smith declared, "There is no other God in Heaven but that God that has flesh and bones."[62] *Doctrine and Covenants* 130:22 teaches, "The Father has a body of flesh and bones as tangible as man's…." McConkie called God "a glorified resurrected Personage having a tangible body of flesh and bones."[63] But Jesus Himself taught that a true "spirit does not have flesh and bones" (Luke 24:39) and therefore, if "God is spirit," He cannot, as Mormons claim, have a tangible physical body as mankind does.

Nevertheless, because Mormonism teaches that its gods are localized and physical, it is not unexpected that they can have sexual intercourse. Mormonism teaches that the gods are sexually active. For all eternity men have been evolving into gods. Once they reach the state of godhood, they sexually beget spirit children with their celestial wives. These spirit children then have an opportunity to inhabit a physical body on a physical earth in order to attain their own godhood and continue the process. McConkie taught:

> We are the offspring of God. He is our eternal father; we have also an eternal mother. There is no such thing as a father without a mother, nor can there be children without parents. We were born as the spirit children of celestial parents long before the foundations of this world were laid.[64]

One reason for early Mormon teaching favoring polygamy is seen in the fact that Mormons were only imitating their gods.[65, 66]

But again, these gods produce spirit children who require physical bodies. Thus, earths are "created" (materially organized) and populated with physical bodies so that the spirit children might have the opportunity to progress to godhood just as their parents did:

> Just as men were first born as spirit children to their Eternal Father and His companion, the children born to resurrected beings are spirit beings and must be sent in their turn to another earth to pass through the trials of mortality and obtain a physical body.[67]

Here we see one of Mormonism's apparent theological rationalizations for the early doctrine of polygamy. If one wife could produce ten bodies for the spirit children to inhabit and thereby have the opportunity to become gods, then 20 wives could produce 200 bodies for these spirits; the more bodies the better; hence, the more wives the better. Brigham Young stated, "The Lord created you and me for the purpose of becoming Gods like Himself....We are created...to become Gods like unto our Father in Heaven" so that we can then create "worlds on worlds."[68] Milton R. Hunter, a member of the First Council of Seventy, taught that "God the Eternal Father was once a mortal man....He became God....He grew in experience and continued to grow until he attained the status of Godhood."[69]

But Mormonism also teaches that its gods were once imperfect, including God the Father and God the Son. That is why even God the Father and Jesus

Christ (two of the gods of this earth) required salvation. If every god was once an imperfect man who was saved through his good works, which exalted him to godhood, then God Himself once required salvation. As Marion G. Romney (1897–1988), a member of the First Presidency, observed, "God is a perfected saved soul enjoying eternal life."[70]

All of this is why the Mormon concept of God cannot possibly be considered Christian. The Mormon Church may claim that Christians are in a state of apostasy and have lost the true knowledge of God, but a careful examination of Mormon teaching on God reveals otherwise. In essence, Mormonism is a religion of pagan polytheism. The concept of physical, sexual, procreating gods defended by the Mormon Church coincides with pagan and occult belief, not Christian belief.

10

What does Mormonism teach about Jesus Christ?

Mormonism claims that it believes in the true, biblical Jesus Christ. Gordon B. Hinckley, fifteenth president of The Church of Jesus Christ of Latter-day Saints, states:

> We are Christians in a very real sense and that is coming to be more and more widely recognized....[People] have come to recognize that we are, and that we have a very vital and dynamic religion based on the teachings of Jesus Christ. We, of course, accept Jesus Christ as our Leader, our King, our Savior. The dominant figure in the history of the world, the only perfect Man who ever walked the earth, the living Son of the living God. He is our Savior and our Redeemer through whose atoning sacrifice has come the opportunity of eternal life.[71]

Right after Hinckley's quote, this statement appears: "Members of [the Church]...pray and worship in the name of Jesus Christ. He is the center of our faith and the head of our Church. The Book of

Mormon is Another Testament of Jesus Christ and witnesses of His divinity, His life, and His Atonement."[72] But consider the following chart contrasting the Mormon Christ (whom it confuses with Jehovah of the Old Testament) with the biblical Christ.

The Mormon Jesus Christ	The Biblical Jesus Christ
A created being; the brother of Lucifer	Uncreated God
Earned his own salvation (exaltation)	As God, Christ required no salvation
Common (one of many gods) and of minor importance in the larger Mormon cosmology	Unique (the Second Person of the one Godhead) and of supreme importance throughout eternity and in all creation
Conceived by the physical sex act of the Father (Adam or Elohim) and Mary	Conceived by the Holy Spirit who overshadowed Mary, a true virgin
A married polygamist?	An unmarried monogamist

The following brief statements by Mormon leaders reveal the true beliefs of the Mormon Church concerning Christ. In essence, the Mormon doctrine of Christ (as with many other of its doctrines) parallels those found in the world of paganism and the occult.

First, Mormonism teaches that Jesus Christ was a created being, not eternal God as the Bible clearly instructs (John 1:1,3; Titus 2:13), and that He was the first and foremost of subsequent billions of spirit children created through sexual intercourse between the male and female earth gods. *Doctrine and Covenants* 93:21-23 teaches that "Christ, the Firstborn, was the mightiest of all the spirit children of the Father." James Talmage affirmed in the standard Mormon church work *The Articles of Faith,* "Among the spirit children of Elohim, the firstborn was and is Jehovah, or Jesus Christ, to whom all others are juniors."[73]

In Mormonism, Jesus is also seen as the brother of Satan. Since Satan was also a preexistent spirit creation of the male and female earth gods, Christ must, therefore, be his relation. Christ and the devil are "blood" brothers. If the devil and his demons were all spirit children of the Mormon earth god "Elohim," it must follow that they, too, are Jesus' brothers, just as they are the brothers of all mankind. As one Mormon writer states, "As for the devil and his fellow spirits, they are brothers to man and also to Jesus and sons and daughters to God in the same sense that we are."[74] In essence then, the difference between Christ and the devil in Mormonism is not one of kind, but only one of degree.

Second, Mormonism teaches that Jesus is a saved being. Because Jesus was only one more spirit offspring of the male and female earth gods (like all men and women), He, too, had to earn His salvation: "Jesus Christ is the Son of God....He came to earth to work out His own salvation....After His resurrection, He gained all power in Heaven."[75] And "by obedience and devotion to the truth, [Jesus] attained that pinnacle of intelligence which ranked Him as a God."[76] This is why McConkie emphasized, "Christ...is a saved being."[77]

Third, in Mormon teaching Jesus Christ is not unique, at least in nature. His divinity is not unique, for every exalted man will attain the same godhood that Christ now experiences. Neither is His incarnation unique; Christ, like all men, is only an incarnated spirit man who, in a preexistent state, was the offspring of sexual union between the male and female earth gods who made Him.

Mormons do refer to Christ as a "greater" being than other spirit children of the male and female earth gods, but only on this earth. Further, Christ is their senior only by priority and position—not nature or essence. In fact, as a spirit child of the earth gods, He *is* of the same exact nature as all men and all

26

demons. This is one reason Mormons refer to Him as their "elder brother." And so, "Jesus is man's spiritual brother. We dwelt with Him in the spirit world as members of that large society of eternal intelligences, which included our Heavenly Parents."[78, 79]

In fact, Christ was unique in nature in only one way—by His physical birth. Rather than having a merely human father as the rest of us on this earth, His mother had physical sex with God (Elohim).[80]

Fourth, as just noted, Mormons accept the birth of Jesus Christ through sexual intercourse between God (Elohim) and Mary. Because "sexuality…is actually an attribute of God…God is a procreating personage of flesh and bone" and "the Holy Ghost was not the father of Jesus."[81] In *Doctrines of Salvation*, Joseph Fielding Smith asserted, "Christ was begotten of God. He was not born without the aid of Man and *that Man was God"!*[82] McConkie declared, "Christ was begotten by an Immortal Father the same way that mortal men are begotten by mortal fathers."[83]

In other words, Mary was married to *both* her earthly husband, Joseph, and God. Brigham Young confessed, "The man Joseph, the husband of Mary, did not, that we know of, have more than one wife, but Mary, the wife of Joseph, had another husband [that is, God]."[84]

Fifth, some Mormons have also taught that Jesus Christ was a polygamist having several wives, another unbiblical doctrine. The early Mormon apostle Orson Pratt claimed that Jesus Christ was married at Cana of Galilee, that Mary and Martha (and others) were His wives, and that He had children. Thus, Jesus was a polygamist who proved it by "marrying many honorable wives."[85]

This, then, is the Mormon Jesus Christ—a sexually created spirit-brother of Lucifer, a possible polygamist, and one of many gods who earned salvation, immortality, and godhood.

Biblically all of this is false. Jesus Christ is God. He is eternal and was, therefore, never created (John 1:1-3; Colossians 1:16,17; Isaiah 9:6; Micah 5:2). Further, Jesus Christ is not the brother of the devil; He came to destroy the works of the devil (1 John 3:8). He was not a man who earned His salvation; He was God who (through the incarnation) died on the cross for man's salvation (1 Peter 2:24). He never married, nor was he born by sexual intercourse between a pagan god and the virgin Mary (John 1).

In fact, not a single biblical Scripture can be advanced by Mormons in defense of any of their teachings on Jesus Christ. Yet Mormon missionaries come to the door and say in full sincerity that they are Christians who believe in the biblical Jesus Christ.

11

What do Mormons teach about salvation and life after death?

Mormon teaching on salvation presents different kinds of salvation leading to different kinds of heaven.

First, there is a *general salvation*, which Mormons call "salvation by grace." Mormonism affirms this occurs to all men. But this general salvation is restricted to resurrection from the dead and immortality; it does not decide a person's specific residence or degree of glory in the next life. This is decided by the second category of Mormon salvation, *individual salvation*. Individual salvation determines which one of the three "heavens" one goes to, and whether or not one earns true "eternal life" (godhood).

General salvation is said to be based on grace while individual salvation is confessedly by good works. Therefore, Mormons may *claim* that they believe salvation is by grace; however, by this, they mean only that every person will be resurrected from the dead. The actual destiny of that person is determined by personal righteousness[86] (see Question 12).

A person's good works and personal merit determine which "kingdom of glory" he or she inherits after death. The lowest kingdom of glory is called the *telestial* kingdom. It is the place of the wicked, where most of humanity will reside. Such persons will be excluded from the presence of God and Christ. The kingdom above this is called the *terrestrial* kingdom of glory. This is where lukewarm Mormons, good non-Mormons, and those who accept Mormonism after death go.

The highest kingdom of glory is the *celestial* kingdom, and this is gained by "complete obedience" to gospel law.[87] This kingdom has three parts, but it is only in the highest part of the celestial kingdom that salvation in its fullest sense is found. Salvation in its truest sense is attaining absolute godhood and eternal sexual increase.[88]

In conclusion, worthy Mormons attain exaltation or deification in the highest heaven of the celestial kingdom. All other people are said to be "damned," which is, in effect, to inherit a restricted and servant status in lesser kingdoms—but "kingdoms" nonetheless.

12

Do Mormons teach that true salvation occurs only by good works and personal righteousness?

From its inception, the Mormon Church has consistently and adamantly opposed the clear biblical teaching of justification by grace through faith alone (Ephesians 2:8,9; Philippians 3:9). In fact, few religions are more hostile to the biblical teaching of salvation by grace than Mormonism. Talmage refers to "a most pernicious doctrine—that of justification by belief alone."[89] Joseph Fielding Smith taught that "mankind [is] damned by [the] 'faith alone' doctrine."[90] McConkie complained, "Many Protestants...erroneously conclude that men are saved by grace alone without doing the works of righteousness."[91]

Because salvation by grace is thoroughly rejected, Mormonism forcefully teaches a system of salvation by works of righteousness and personal merit. Both the Book of Mormon and *Doctrine and Covenants* teach

29

"works salvation."[92] Further, virtually every Mormon authority of past and present has emphasized the absolute necessity of salvation by works and personal righteousness.

Heber C. Kimball taught, "I have power to save myself, and if I do not save myself, who will save me? All have that privilege, and naught can save us but obedience to the commandments of God."[93] Talmage referred to "the absolute requirement of individual compliance with the laws and ordinances of his [Jesus'] gospel by which salvation may be attained."[94] Joseph Fielding Smith emphasized that "the new birth is also a matter of obedience to law."[95] Bruce McConkie believed that the great defender of justification by faith alone, the apostle Paul, is "the apostle of good works, of personal righteousness, of keeping the commandments, of pressing forward with a steadfastness in Christ, of earning the right to eternal life by the obedience to the laws and ordinances of the gospel."[96]

But, again, none of this is biblical teaching. From the Old Testament to the Gospels and the book of Acts, from the apostle Paul's writings to the apostle John's, the Bible teaches only one way of salvation—by grace through faith alone. "Of Him [Jesus], all the prophets bear witness that through His name everyone who believes in Him receives forgiveness of sins" (Acts 10:43).

Jesus Himself taught that salvation was secured by faith alone. For example, "Truly, truly, I say to you, he who hears My word, and believes Him who sent Me, has eternal life, and does not come into judgment, but has passed out of death into life" (John 5:24). "Truly, truly, I say to you, he who believes has eternal life" (John 6:47). "Jesus answered and said to them, 'This is the work of God, that you believe in Him whom He has sent'" (John 6:29).

Notice the testimony of the following additional Scriptures. As early as Genesis we read, "Abram believed the Lord, and he credited it to him as righteousness" (Genesis 15:6 NIV). The apostle Paul comments on this verse when he asserts, "What does the

Scripture say? 'Abraham believed God and it was credited to him as righteousness'" (Romans 4:3 NIV). Paul never once taught that salvation was earned by good works and personal righteousness, as Mormons claim. To maintain this is to seriously misinterpret and distort Paul's teaching. In his own words, Paul confessed that even though he was a righteous man according to the law, he counted it

> but rubbish in order that I may gain Christ, and may be found in Him, not having a righteousness of my own derived from the Law, but that which is through faith in Christ, the righteousness which comes from God on the basis of faith (Philippians 3:8-9).

Does this sound as though Paul was a great defender of salvation by good works and of "earning the right to salvation" by obedience to gospel law? To the contrary, Paul repeatedly emphasized salvation was secured by grace through faith in Christ alone, as the following Scriptures prove:

> For we maintain that a man is justified by faith apart from works of the Law (Romans 3:28).
>
> By grace you have been saved through faith; and that not of yourselves, it is the gift of God; not as a result of works, that no one should boast (Ephesians 2:8,9).
>
> But if it is by grace, it is no longer on the basis of works, otherwise grace is no longer grace (Romans 11:6).
>
> I do not nullify the grace of God; for if righteousness comes through the Law, then Christ died needlessly (Galatians 2:21; see also Romans 4:5,6; 10:4; Galatians 3:11; Titus 3:5).

Mormonism, because it teaches a religious system of salvation by good works and personal righteousness, comes under the condemnation so clearly expressed by the apostle Paul in Galatians 1:8 (NIV):

> But even if we or an angel from heaven should preach a gospel other than the one we preached to you, let him be eternally condemned!

If Mormonism teaches personal salvation by good works and individual merit, then of what value was the atonement of Jesus Christ for our sins?

13

What does Mormonism teach about the atoning death of Jesus Christ on the cross?

Mormonism claims that "salvation comes because of the atonement."[97] In spite of such claims, the Mormon Church does not believe in the biblical atonement, but rather in an atonement of its own devising. The value of the atonement in Mormon thinking is that it gives men the *opportunity* to earn their own salvation through personal merit.

For the individual Mormon, righteousness by works would avail nothing if the atonement had not canceled the penalty of Adam's sin, which brought physical death to every man.[98] Mormons are grateful for the atonement because it raises them from the dead—but this is all it does. Mormons believe that "...the Lord died in order to bring about the resurrection of the dead."[99]

In other words, in no way has Christ's death actually purchased full salvation for anyone.[100, 101]

Just as a college degree does not secure a salary but only makes earning one possible, so Christ's death does not secure salvation but only makes earning it possible by good works. In Mormonism, the actual *saving value* of the atonement is virtually nonexistent. In fact, Mormonism has such a low view of the atonement that during its early history, the Church taught that men must have their own blood shed (be killed) in order to atone for certain sins.[102] Unfortunately, there is little doubt that many individuals were actually murdered in the mistaken belief that this would allegedly atone for their sins and send them to heaven.[103] Mormon leaders such as C.W. Penrose have taught that the idea that Christ's death is sufficient for salvation is "the great error" and most pernicious delusion of Christianity.[104]

But the teaching of the Bible is clear: The death of Christ on the cross actually *paid the penalty for all sin*. In order to appropriate that forgiveness, all any person need do is believe on the Lord Jesus Christ as these Scriptures (emphases added) show.

> Believe in the Lord Jesus Christ and you *shall* be saved... (Acts 16:31).
> For I delivered to you as of first importance what I also received, that Christ *died for our sins* according to the Scriptures (1 Corinthians 15:3).
> In Him we have redemption *through His blood, the forgiveness of our trespasses*, according to the riches of His grace (Ephesians 1:7).
> He Himself *bore our sins in His body on the cross* that we might die to sin and live to righteousness; for by His wounds you were healed (1 Peter 2:24).
> He forgave us *all* our sins (Colossians 2:13).

In essence, Mormonism completely opposes the saving value of Christ's death on the cross. It tells men and women that their good works will save them, forgive their sins, and bring them to heaven. But in doing this, it rejects the most fundamental teaching of the Bible and all Christian faith. When Mormonism teaches men to trust in a false gospel, again this teaching comes under the judgment of God Himself (Galatians 1:6-8).

One thing should be obvious from this discussion of Mormon beliefs—Mormon faith and Christian faith are not the same. Mormonism rejects and opposes the clear biblical teaching concerning God, Jesus Christ, salvation, the death of Christ, and so on down the list. It denies the biblical teaching on man, faith, the Fall, death and the afterlife, the Bible, the Holy Spirit, and many other doctrines.[105]

In conclusion, those people who claim that Mormons are brothers or sisters in Christ or that Mormonism is a Christian religion are simply wrong. Mormonism opposes almost every biblical doctrine and, therefore, cannot possibly be considered Christian.

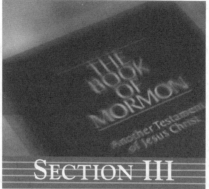

Section III

Mormonism—A Critical Evaluation

> If a faith will not bear to be investigated; if its
> preachers and professors are afraid to have it
> examined, their foundation must be very
> weak.[106]

> —George A. Smith
> Mormon apostle and historian

Few religions have such a wealth of historical, archaeological, and other data arrayed against them as the Mormon religion. In this section, we will briefly examine some of this data, which prove that Mormon claims are false. We will also show why it is impossible to examine this evidence fairly and then conclude that the Mormon Church is a divine revelation and represents the one true church of God on earth.

14

Was there a universal apostasy by the early Christian Church?

The Mormon Church claims that the original teachings of Christ and the apostles reflected a Mormon worldview. However, the early church soon apostatized and was only restored through Joseph Smith 1800 years later.[107, 108]

The Mormon Church never has (and never will) establish 1) that a universal apostasy occurred or 2) that the original gospel was Mormon. It can be historically demonstrated there was no universal apostasy, and it can be proven to anyone's satisfaction that the beliefs of Jesus and the apostles as recorded in the New Testament have not been corrupted.[109] The Mormon claim to being a restored church is demonstrably false. Without an apostasy, nothing existed to be restored (Matthew 16:18; 24:35; Ephesians 3:21; Hebrews 12:28; Romans 9:29; 11:4,5).

15

Is the "first vision" account forming the foundation of the Mormon Church really credible?

Joseph Smith's "first vision" forms the essence of Mormonism's claim to uniqueness: that God Himself had rejected all other churches as false and was now restoring the "true" church through this 15-year-old boy.[110] This is why Mormons have agreed that the "first vision" account is absolutely crucial to the credibility and authority of both Smith and the Church. Second in importance only to Christ's "deity," the "first vision" is the "foundation of the church"; the Mormon Church stands or falls on the authenticity of this event, and the "truth and validity" of all of Joseph Smith's subsequent work rests upon its genuineness.[111] The following facts prove, by Mormonism's own assertions, that their church is based on falsehood.

The official account of the event was written by Smith around 1838 and published in *Times and Seasons* in 1842, two decades after "the event" took place.[112] What most Mormons have never been told is that at least five *earlier* drafts of the "first vision" exist. These conflicting accounts have been ignored or repressed by Mormon leaders because they disagree with what has come to be the preferred or official version. Of all versions, the official composition, Smith's final draft, is the least credible.[113]

The earliest known account was written by Smith in 1832. It varies in important details with the official version. There are discrepancies in Smith's age, the presence of an evil power, Smith's reason for seeking the Lord, the existence of a revival, and the number of divine personages in the vision.

For example, the revival Smith claimed happened in 1820 (he clearly gives his age as 15) actually took place in 1824–1825.[114] There was no revival in 1820, and, therefore, Smith had no reason to seek God's counsel over his own religious confusion.

Another account by Smith was written between 1835–1836.[115] In this different and contradictory version, there is no mention of God or Christ, but only of many spirits and "angels" who testified of Jesus.

Leading authorities on Mormonism Jerald and Sandra Tanner conclude:

> We have now examined three different handwritten manuscripts of the first vision. They were all written by Joseph Smith or his scribes and yet every one of them is different. The first account says there was only one personage. The second account says there were many, and the third says there were two. The church, of course, accepts the version which accepts two personages....At any rate...it becomes very difficult to believe that Joseph Smith ever had a vision in the grove.[116]

The crucial "first vision" account is simply not credible. Mormons who accept it must ignore and deny strong evidence to the contrary.*

16

What intractable problems face the Book of Mormon?

Dr. Hugh Nibley, considered by many Mormons to be one of the greatest scholars in the Church, declares: "The Book of Mormon can and should be tested. It invites criticism."[118] Tenth president Joseph Fielding Smith said that the evidence for it "internally and externally is overwhelming."[119]

But unfortunately, the only evidence is overwhelmingly negative.

---

* The reader may pursue the issue of various vision accounts in *Dialogue: A Journal of Mormon Thought*, Autumn 1966 and Spring 1971 issues; *Brigham Young University Studies*, Spring 1969 and elsewhere.[117] We also note that as a whole, Smith's vision/visions were not as unique as claimed by Mormon authorities. In fact, they fit a characteristic pattern of spiritistic contacts that have occurred throughout history. There is no doubt that Smith was subject to spiritistic visions and inspiration; what must be doubted is the authenticity and relevance of the official version of the Mormon Church.

First, although the Church denies it, there is little doubt that, given Smith's claims, the Book of Mormon was translated by occult means.[120] Smith put a magical "seer" stone into a hat, and then buried his face in the hat to exclude the light. Next, words in "reformed Egyptian" (no such language is known to exist) magically appeared with their translation, and Smith spoke the translation to a scribe who wrote it down. One of Smith's many wives, Emma Smith, confesses: "In writing for your father, I frequently wrote day after day....He sitting with his face buried in his hat, with a stone in it, and dictating hour after hour...."[121]

In addition, the very content of the Book of Mormon makes it impossible to accept it as a divine revelation. The Book of Mormon claims to be a *translation* of ancient writings on gold plates. These plates were supposedly written at least 1,400 years ago and detailed the history of the Jewish "Nephites" from 600 B.C. through A.D. 421. But it is virtually impossible that records written 1,400 years prior to the time of Joseph Smith should detail specific social, political, and religious concerns unique to nineteenth-century America.

In a scholarly work for which she was excommunicated from the Mormon Church (*No Man Knows My History: The Life of Joseph Smith*), Fawn Brodie discusses the reasons supporting a nineteenth-century origin for the Book of Mormon.[122] In a similar fashion, one of the first able reviews of the Book of Mormon commented:

> This prophet Smith, through his stone spectacles, wrote on the plates of Nephi in his Book of Mormon every error and almost every truth discussed in New York for the last ten years.[123]

Why would 1,400- to 2,400-year-old records deal with distinctly nineteenth-century theological and political disputes? This is certainly puzzling unless, of course, they were not 1,400 to 2,400 years old. Even noted Mormon historian B.H. Roberts confessed that

Joseph Smith alone could have written the Book of Mormon.[124]

But the content of the Book of Mormon presents further difficulties. For example, there are many clearly demonstrated plagiarisms. Material has been taken from Ethan Smith's *View of the Hebrews* (1823), a book that was available to Joseph Smith,[125] as well as from the King James Bible. Some 27,000 words from the King James Bible are found in the Book of Mormon.[126]

But if the Book of Mormon was first written between 600 B.C. and A.D. 421, how could it possibly contain such extensive quotations from the King James Bible, not to be written for another 1,200 to 2,000 years? The Tanners have listed, one by one, 400 verses and portions of verses quoted from the New Testament in the Book of Mormon in their book *The Case Against Mormonism*.[127]

The Book of Mormon even contains King James Bible *translation errors*. For example, in 2 Nephi 14:5 (Isaiah 4:5) the correct translation of the Hebrew *chupaah* is "canopy," not "defense." In 2 Nephi 15:25 (Isaiah 5:25) the correct translation of the Hebrew *suchah* is "refuse," not "torn."

Another problem for the Book of Mormon is archaeology, a major embarrassment to the Mormon Church. Mormon missionaries continue to claim that the science of archaeology substantiates the Book of Mormon, but whether we consider the alleged cities, persons, animals, fabrics, metals, wars and war implements, kings, palaces, or crops, all the evidence points to their nonexistence. Gordon Fraser comments:

> Mormon archaeologists have been trying for years to establish some evidence that will confirm the presence of the [Mormon] church in America. There is still not a scintilla of evidence, either in the religious philosophy of the ancient writings or in the presence of artifacts, that lead to such a belief.[128]

To show how embarrassing this situation is, consider that Mormon missionaries often claim that the Smithsonian Institution or other professional organizations have utilized the Book of Mormon as an archaeological guide. In fact, the Smithsonian Institution has received so many inquiries concerning this that they actually return a standard form-letter denying it. The first of many points they make in their rebuttal of Mormon claims is, "The Smithsonian Institution has never used the Book of Mormon in any way as a scientific guide. Smithsonian archaeologists see no direct connection between the archaeology of the New World and the subject matter of the book."[129] Further, its Bureau of American Ethnology asserts, "There is no evidence whatever of any migration from Israel to America, and likewise no evidence that pre-Columbian Indians had any knowledge of Christianity or the Bible."[130]

Even the prestigious National Geographic Society has flatly denied Mormon missionary claims:

> With regard to the cities mentioned in *The Book of Mormon*, neither representatives of the National Geographic Society nor archaeologists connected with any other institution of equal prestige have ever used *The Book of Mormon* in locating historic ruins in Middle America or elsewhere.[131]

No Book of Mormon cities have ever been located, no Book of Mormon person, place, nation, or name has been found, no Book of Mormon artifacts, no Book of Mormon scriptures, no Book of Mormon inscriptions, no Book of Mormon gold plates— nothing that demonstrates the Book of Mormon is anything other than myth or invention has *ever* been found.

By contrast, the archaeological evidence for the Bible is so convincing that even a former skeptic such as the great archaeologist Sir William Ramsey became converted to Christian belief. But the archaeological evidence against Mormon claims is so devastating that prominent Mormon archaeologist Thomas Stewart Ferguson quit the Mormon Church and repudiated its prophet.[132]

In conclusion, anyone who wishes can prove to their own satisfaction that the Book of Mormon cannot possibly be divinely inspired. Its occult method of translation, plagiarisms, internal inconsistences, archaeological lack of verification, and many other problems reveal that the Mormon Church is in serious error when it claims otherwise.[133]

17

Are the Mormon scriptures really the Word of God? If so, why has the Church made significant changes in them; why do they contain demonstrable errors and undeniable contradictions?

The Mormon Church claims that the Book of Mormon, *The Pearl of Great Price*, and *Doctrine and Covenants* are genuine scriptures inspired by God. But this cannot possibly be true.

The Tanners have reprinted the original 1830 edition of the Book of Mormon, noting in the text significant changes and more than 3,000 minor changes. But even a single minor change is incompatible with its claimed word-by-word translation.[134] For example, the 1830 edition of Mosiah 21:28 refers to King Benjamin, while modern editions read "King Mosiah." According to the Book of Mormon chronology, Benjamin was no longer king at the time (he was dead: Mosiah 6:3-7; 7:1), so the inspired name was changed to read King Mosiah to cover the error.

Similarly, serious doctrinal problems have been corrected. For example, in 1 Nephi 11:18 the 1830 edition teaches, "The virgin which thou seest, is the mother of God, after the manner of the flesh." However, since Mary could not literally be the mother of the earth deity "Elohim," modern editions read "the mother of the Son of God" rather than "the mother of God."

Other significant errors include the Book of Mormon teaching that Jesus was born in Jerusalem (Alma 7:9-10), not in Bethlehem as the Bible teaches (Micah 5:2; Matthew 2:1). In Helaman 14:20, during Jesus' crucifixion, the darkness over the face of the land is said to have lasted for three *days* instead of the biblical three *hours* (Matthew 27:45; Mark 15:33).

We have two choices: Either Smith copied errors that were originally on the supposed gold plates or the Book of Mormon is not "a perfect translation by the power of God" as Mormonism claims. Either way, the Book of Mormon cannot be trusted.

The Mormon scripture *Doctrine and Covenants* presents more serious problems. The original edition of *Doctrine and Covenants* was called the *Book of Commandments* and was published in 1833. This book contained allegedly direct, word-for-word revelations from God to Joseph Smith. But in 1835 the *Book of Commandments* was reissued under the title *Doctrine and Covenants* and had, literally, *thousands* of changes made from "God's" earlier revelations. There are at least 65,000 changes between the *Book of Commandments* and *Doctrine and Covenants*. Joseph Smith apparently made mistakes that "God" missed when He stopped the translation process to correct scribal errors.[135]

Nevertheless, the Mormon Church frequently claims that the Book of Mormon and *Doctrine and Covenants* have never been changed. Supposedly, there has been no tampering with "God's Word."[136] But the evidence is there for anyone to see. All interested readers may examine the issue for themselves by comparing modern versions with the first editions of the Book of Mormon and *Doctrine and Covenants* as found in *Joseph Smith Begins His Work*, Volumes 1 and 2 (notarized photostat copies).[137]

The third inspired scripture of the Mormon Church is *The Pearl of Great Price*. The Church also maintains this book has not undergone changes. And yet again there are literally thousands of words deleted and hundreds of words added during reprints. The Tanner's text *Changes in The Pearl of Great Price: A*

Photo Reprint of the Original 1851 Edition of The Pearl of Great Price with All the Changes Marked proves this beyond doubt.[138]

Further, a portion of *The Pearl of Great Price*, "The Book of Abraham," has recently been proven a forgery. It is a copy of a pagan text—the Egyptian *Book of Breathings*, an extension of the occult Egyptian *Book of the Dead* relating to the alleged journeys of the soul after death.[139] The Mormon Church refuses to acknowledge its fabrication because to do so is to confess that Joseph Smith cannot be trusted in the most vital area of all—his ability to reveal the Word of God. Smith claimed that he translated both "The Book of Abraham" and the Book of Mormon under the power of God. But since "The Book of Abraham" is now a proven forgery of a pagan text, how can any Mormon know that the Book of Mormon is not a similar fabrication?[140]

The Book of Mormon, *Doctrine and Covenants*, and *The Pearl of Great Price* are the "Word of God" to Mormons. Yet they have been changed in hundreds and even thousands of places—corrections, additions, deletions—all done without any indication or acknowledgment of such action.[141, 142] Why has this been done if these books are truly the Word of God? Why have Mormon leaders kept such actions hidden from Church members?[143]

18

What is the irreconcilable dilemma for the individual Mormon?

The irreconcilable dilemma for the individual Mormon is the same found in all nonbiblical, spiritistic inspiration: contradictory revelation. (See Questions 21-23.) On some very vital issues, modern Mormon prophets have contradicted and even denied teachings by earlier Mormon prophets![144]

Where does this leave the average Mormon? Should he or she accept the Church's claim that the early prophets *were* indeed prophets and authoritative? If so, then he or she must charge modern Mormonism with apostasy, for the modern Church absolutely denies many of its early, crucial divine revelations. Or should the average Mormon discard the early Mormon prophets as men who received erroneous revelations and were, therefore, false prophets, since many of their teachings are rejected today by Church leadership? If so, then the entire Mormon Church collapses, for it is based squarely on the divine *authority* of such men.

In the end, the individual Mormon is faced with two equally unpleasant options. Either 1) the modern Mormon Church is in apostasy and cannot be trusted; or 2) the early prophets were deceivers or deceived men and cannot be trusted. (See Question 20.)

19

If the Mormon prophets were divinely inspired, how does the Mormon Church explain their false prophecies?

In his own words Joseph Smith Jr. emphasized:

> The only way of ascertaining a true prophet is to compare his prophecies with the ancient Word of God, and see if they agree....When, therefore, any man, no matter who, or how high his standing may be, utters, or publishes, anything that afterwards proves to be untrue, he is a false prophet.[145]

Bruce McConkie agrees and claims, "By their works it shall be known whether professing ministers of religion are true or false prophets. Joseph Smith was a true prophet."[146]

But the Mormon Church also admits that "if his claims to divine appointment be false, forming as they do the foundation of the Church in this last dispensation, the superstructure [of the Church] cannot be stable."[147]

If Smith did give false prophecies, then the super-structure of the Mormon Church collapses. According to Deuteronomy 18:20-22, if an alleged prophet's prophecy did not come true, he spoke in the name of the Lord presumptuously. But if this prophet spoke in the names of *false gods* to lead the people astray, that prophet was to die.

Joseph Smith claimed to be a true biblical prophet. The fact that his prophecies did not come true proves he was a false prophet. He spoke in the name of *false gods* and taught false doctrines, thereby leading people astray from biblical truth.

In *Doctrine and Covenants* 1:37,38, "God" promises that the prophecies and promises within the book's pages "shall all be fulfilled." *Doctrine and Covenants* 84:1-5,31, declares under the authority of "the Word of the Lord" that both a city and a temple are to be built "in the Western boundaries of the State of Missouri and dedicated by the hand of Joseph Smith." This was a revelation given to Smith on September 22-23, 1832, at Independence, MO. It stated clearly that the temple would be erected during the lifetime of those then living. The prophecy promised the temple would be erected "in this generation" (*Doctrine & Covenants* 84:4,5), and that "this generation shall not all pass away" until it was built.

In 1864, 30 years after the prophecy was given, the apostle George Cannon continued to teach that the temple would be built before "this generation" passed away.[148] In 1870, almost 40 years later, Orson Pratt confirmed that the Church could expect a literal fulfillment of the prophecy because "God promised it" and "God cannot lie."[149] In 1900, 70 years later, Lorenzo Snow emphasized that the Mormons now living in Utah would still go back to Missouri and build their temple.[150] Even in 1931, 99 years after the prophecy, Joseph Fielding Smith was stating his "firm belief" that the temple would be built.[151]

But more than 170 years after the original prophecy, the temple has still not been built! "This generation" all passed away long ago. Joseph Smith is also long since dead and unable to dedicate the temple as "God" promised. No one can deny the prophecy was false.*

Another false prediction can be seen in the so-called "Civil War" prophecy recorded in *Doctrine and Covenants* 87:1-8, given on December 25, 1832. Although Mormons claim the prediction is "remarkable" and proof of Smith's prophethood, this is not the case. First, the prediction of a civil war to begin in South Carolina was not unusual. In 1832 Congress passed a tariff act refused by South Carolina, and Andrew Jackson alerted the troops. Even in 1832 "the nation was fully expecting a war to begin promptly in South Carolina."[152]

Also, the prophecy itself is wrong on a number of counts. For one thing, when the Civil War did occur, it was not poured out upon "all nations." There were no earthquakes, "thunder of heaven," or lightning. Neither did all the earth's population feel the "wrath of the Almighty" nor was there "a full end of all nations." In addition, there is some doubt the prophecy was a genuine prediction to begin with.[153]

Mormon rationalizations for these and numerous other false prophecies[154] have proved futile. Instead of admitting the fact that Smith was a false prophet, Mormons continue to deceive other people by portraying him as a genuine prophet of God.

20

Why has the Mormon Church ignored the compelling historical research of Jerald and Sandra Tanner and others?

Jerald and Sandra Tanner, former Mormons, have produced a small library of careful historical research that casts grave doubt upon almost all the major claims of the Mormon Church.

---

* The Community of Christ, formerly the Reorganized Church of Jesus Christ of Latter Day Saints, built a temple *across the street* from the temple lot on which Joseph Smith Jr. laid a cornerstone for the prophesied temple.

46

The question is, Why has the Mormon Church ignored compelling historical research? Why has the Church acted almost as if it doesn't even exist? This issue is important, indeed vital, because the Church claims to be concerned about the truth—yet continues to reject a wealth of factual data having critical bearing on Mormon origins, history, doctrine, scripture, and censorship.

Mormonia: A Quarterly Bibliography of Works on Mormonism called the Tanners' book *Shadow or Reality?* "perhaps the most exhaustive exposé of Mormonism between two covers."[155] Jennings G. Olson, professor of philosophy at Webber College observed it was "the most comprehensive and thorough analysis and evaluation of Mormonism ever produced in the history of the Church."[156] Dr. Gordon Fraser accurately described it as "an encyclopedia of Mormonism's lack of credibility."[157]

If indisputable historical documents have been found discrediting Mormon beliefs, it deeply concerns all Mormon people. Mormons, especially Mormon leaders, should want to look into this if they are as concerned with the truth as they say.

We vigorously encourage interested readers to secure a list of materials (offered at cost) from Utah Lighthouse Ministry, PO Box 1884, Salt Lake City, Utah 84110 and www.utlm.org. Mormons have a right to this information even if the Church disagrees.

What may we conclude to this point? Even with so brief a treatment as found in this book, there is little doubt that Mormonism is not what proponents claim. Mormonism cannot possibly be a revelation from the biblical God since it denies the nature of God Himself as revealed in the Bible and also distorts nearly every major biblical doctrine. It cannot possibly be the one true church of Christ on earth because it rejects and distorts the true person of Christ as found in the historical Gospel records. Further, its "first vision" account is not credible; its scriptures—the Book of Mormon, *Doctrine and Covenants* and *The Pearl of Great Price*—also lack credibility on numerous accounts. Joseph Smith himself could not have been a prophet of God because no one can logically deny that he engaged in false prophecy.

If neither Joseph Smith nor the Mormon scriptures are credible, what remains of Mormonism? In essence, no one familiar with the canons of evidence can logically deny that Mormonism must be considered a false religion.

SECTION IV

Mormonism and the Occult:

Should Mormonism Be Considered an Occult Religion?

21

How important is the concept of inspiration and revelation within the Mormon Church?

In Question 2 we saw that Mormonism was founded upon alleged revelations given to Joseph Smith. Throughout its history the Mormon Church has stressed the importance of accepting supernatural revelations.[158]

Mormonism accepts revelation on two levels: 1) canonical (the acceptance of new scripture) and 2) individual (personal, supernatural guidance).

As far as the Church is concerned, "The canon of scripture is still open; many lines, many precepts, are yet to be added; revelation, surpassing in importance and glorious fullness any that has been recorded, is yet to be given to the Church and declared to the world."[159] This is the basis upon which the Church accepted three volumes in addition to the Bible as scripture—the Book of Mormon, *Doctrine and Covenants*, and *The Pearl of Great Price*. In fact, to deny continuous revelation, as Protestantism generally does, is, according to Mormonism, a "heresy and blasphemous denial" of God Himself.[160]

In addition to the importance of revealed scripture, the Church teaches the urgency of personal revelation from God for both Mormon leadership and laity. Without this, one cannot, allegedly, discern God's work from Satan's or truth from error. Hence, the necessity of individual "divine" guidance is also actively stressed.[161] Such revelation may involve an audible voice from God, supernatural dreams, the use of angelic messengers, or communication from the dead, etc.[162]

Mormons assert that direct revelation from God is guiding Church leadership on a daily basis: "The Spirit is giving direct and daily revelation to the presiding Brethren in the administration of the affairs of the church."[163]

Bruce McConkie further emphasized that every good Mormon also receives revelation from God and that it is the duty of Mormons to "gain personal revelation and guidance for their personal affairs."[164]

This concept of individual and corporate revelation is crucial for understanding how Mormonism was led into occult practices and unbiblical doctrines historically. Once the safeguards of biblical authority were rejected, once an uncritical openness to supernatural revelation was accepted,[165] the fate of the Church was sealed. Mormonism could only become an occult religion.

Indeed, the occult philosophy of many spiritistic mediums resembles the revelations given to Smith and other Mormon prophets (including the importance of revelations from the "dead," personal ministry to the dead [proxy-baptism], the doctrine of preexistence, polytheism, different levels of postmortem existence and schooling on the spirit plane, man as God, eternal progression, etc.).

All this is why no less an authority than the late Walter Martin observed, "Occultism in Mormon theology is undeniable."[166] Jerald and Sandra Tanner also document occultism in *Mormonism, Magic and Masonry; Joseph Smith and Money Digging;* and other works.[167]

22

Was Joseph Smith an occultist?

No one can deny that Joseph Smith was an occultist. Dr. Martin observes that "what most Mormons do not recognize is the fact that Joseph Smith was an occultist, and that Mormonism had occultic origins."[168] As is true for many practitioners, both Smith's parents were involved in the occult.[169] This may have brought Joseph a kind of hereditary transference and/or predisposition to psychic ability.[170] Smith claims he received his first supernatural visitation of "angels" at the age of 14.[171]

Smith also had occult powers and, along with a number of other early Mormon leaders,[172] was involved in various occult practices. (In 1826, he was arrested, tried, and found guilty of fortune-telling in Bainbridge, New York.)[173] Smith employed what he called a "Jupiter Talisman"—an amulet supposedly possessing supernatural powers intended to bring wealth, influence, and power to its possessor.[174] He would also place "peepstones" or "seer" stones into a hat, place his face into the hat, and see visions of buried treasure, lost property, etc.[175] As we have seen, this was the method by which the *Book of Mormon* was allegedly translated.[176]

But such activities are simply a variation upon the occult practice of crystal gazing. Further, they are similar to other practices such as occult psychometry and radionics. Nor was Smith alone in his use of seer stones and amulets. The early Mormon people were also prone to use them as means to contact and commune with the spirit world.[177] Even today, many Mormons continue to contact the spirit world to receive guidance and instruction (see Question 23).

That Smith had occult powers and may also have had a number of spirit guides is not surprising.[178] Like mediums and spiritists in general, he had personal experience that the so-called dead "are not far from us, and know and understand our thoughts, feelings and emotions…" and that they could play an important role in spiritual encouragement and growth.[179] Both he and Brigham Young believed that "we have more friends behind the veil than on this side," and that knowledge of the spirit world was crucial to personal salvation.[180]

Smith taught, "The greatest responsibility in this world that God has laid upon us is to seek after our dead," and "those Saints who neglect it [baptism for the dead], in behalf of their deceased relatives, do so at the peril of their own salvation."[181] Thus, "work for the dead is an important determining factor in the Latter-day Saints' attempt to attain their ultimate salvation and exaltation in the Kingdom of God."[182]

23

How frequently do spiritistic revelations occur within Mormonism? How often are the dead contacted?

Given its theology, Mormon interest in seeking the spirits of the dead is logical, and spiritistic revelations and contacts occur somewhat frequently within Mormonism. One major Church teaching is that the spirits of the dead can be assisted and even saved in the next life by work done on their behalf under the auspices of the Mormon Church. How did the Mormon Church adopt such beliefs? From the spirits themselves.

> 1) From its inception Mormonism accepted spiritistic revelations from the dead and other spirits.
>
> 2) Part of these revelations from the spirits concerned the importance of contacting the dead in order to assist them spiritually.
>
> 3) As a result, contacting the dead became a theological necessity within the Mormon Church.

However, in Deuteronomy 18:10-12 (NIV), God commands His people to avoid all forms of contact with the dead: "Let no one be found among you…who practices divination or sorcery…engages in witchcraft, or casts spells, or who is a medium or spiritist or who consults the dead. Anyone who does these things is detestable to the LORD…."

In spite of this warning, the dead have always played a major role in the practice of Mormonism. Both Smith and many subsequent leaders in the Mormon Church were in regular contact with the spirit world.[183] When dead family members or biblical personalities appeared to Joseph Smith, he welcomed them.[184] A sermon delivered by Mormon Elder Parley Pratt in 1853 (five years after the celebrated spiritist movement began in America) indicates early Mormon acceptance of Joseph Smith as a "divine" medium. Jesus Christ was given the role of a spiritistic mediator, and spiritism was to be practiced in the Mormon temple. Pratt gloried in Joseph Smith's role as a spirit medium:

> Who communicated with our great modern Prophet, and revealed through him as a medium, the ancient history of a hemisphere, and the records of the ancient dead? [i.e., who revealed the Book of Mormon? The spirit] Moroni, who had lived on the earth 1400 years before....
>
> Who ordained our first founders to the Apostleship, to hold the keys of the Kingdom of God, and these the times of restoration? Peter, James, and John from the eternal [spirit] world. Who instructed him in the mysteries of the kingdom?...Angels and spirits from the eternal worlds. The Lord has ordained that...conversations and correspondence with God, angels, and spirits, shall be had only in the sanctuary of His holy temple on the earth....One of the leading or fundamental truths of Mormon philosophy [is] that the living may hear from the dead.[185]

Temple spiritism is also noted by Walter Martin, who cited Mormon theologian Charles Penrose in *Mormon Doctrine:* "The temple where the ordinances can be administered for the dead, is a place to hear from the dead. The Priesthood in the flesh, when it is necessary, will receive communications from the priesthood behind the veil [the dead]."[186]

The sixth president of the Church, Joseph F. Smith, continued to support spiritistic/mediumistic contacts within the Church:

> Our father and mothers, brothers, sisters and friends who have passed away from this earth, having been faithful...may have a mission given them to visit their relatives and friends upon the earth again, bringing from the divine Presence messages of love, of warning, or of reproof and instruction....[187]

In harmony with the tradition of occultism in general, many Mormon leaders have claimed they have received spiritistic contacts from dead "spiritual authorities"—Joseph Smith, Brigham Young, other Church presidents, etc.[188, 189, 190]

But if Mormon visitations from the spirit world bring unbiblical teachings (as we have documented), how are they different from any other spiritistic circles that claim visitation by the dead, such as Sun Myung Moon's Unification Church or various "Christian" spiritualist churches? These also bring unbiblical revelations that expose them as demonic deceptions (1 Timothy 4:1), as many former mediums have openly confessed.[191]

How does Mormonism justify its practice of contacting the dead? In harmony with much "Christian" parapsychology and religious spiritualism, the Mormon Church erects a false division between "godly" and "satanic" spirit contact. Allegedly, all Mormon contact with the dead is "godly" practice.

But biblically there is no such division nor can Mormonism justify one. There is no biblically endorsed practice involving "godly" contact with the dead, or "godly" mediumism, "godly" channeling or spiritism; it is *all* classified as an abomination to God (Deuteronomy 18:9-13). The Mormon practice of contacting the dead is little different—in nature or consequence—than similar practices found in the world of the occult. Nor is there any doubt that the spirits who claim to be the dead are really lying spirits the Bible identifies as demons.[192]

Nevertheless, there are many books by Mormons that recount temple manifestations of dead family members as truly "faith-promoting" experiences. Joseph Heinerman's books *Spirit World Manifestations*, *Eternal Testimonies*, and *Temple Manifestations* detail scores of stories of dead family relatives and other spirits instructing Mormon leaders, missionaries, and laymen in genealogical and other Mormon work. In fact, these and other books reveal that for many Mormons, "true" religion involves not only ministering to the spirits of the dead by proxy baptism, but also receiving guidance and instruction from spirits of the dead for spiritual growth.[193] Heinerman states:

> The inhabitants of the spirit world have received special permission to visit their mortal descendants and

assist them and impress upon their minds the primary importance of assimilating genealogical information and performing vicarious ordinance work in the temples.

Spirit world manifestations and angelic appearances have played and continue to play a major role in the upbuilding of God's Kingdom [i.e., Mormonism] in these latter days....

It should be gratifying to Latter-day Saints that those in the spirit world have expressed an intense interest and are increasingly concerned with the activities of God's people upon the earth.[194]

Mormon theologian Duane S. Crowther teaches standard Mormon belief when he says that "good" spirits return to the earth and converse with Mormons to:

1) give counsel

2) give comfort

3) obtain or give information

4) serve as guardian angels

5) prepare others for death

6) summon mortals into the spirit world

7) escort the dying through the veil of death[195]

Such teaching is in complete harmony with the teachings of mediums and spiritists everywhere. Indeed, at this point it is impossible to distinguish Mormon practice from general spiritism.

In conclusion, there is no doubt that Mormonism is a spiritistic, occult religion. It has an occult origin, promotes occult theology and philosophy, and continues to promote occult practices such as contact with the dead.

24

What is the true basis of eternal life, and how is it found?

Biblically, eternal life with God and Christ begins the moment a person receives the true Jesus Christ as his or her personal Savior from sin: "Yet to all who received him, to those who believed in his name, he gave the right to become children of God" (John 1:12 NIV).

It is impossible for anyone to inherit eternal life based on his or her own good works and personal righteousness because no one can ever be good enough to satisfy God's perfect standards. According to the Bible, such persons will only inherit eternal judgment (Matthew 25:46; John 8:24; Galatians 3:21,24).

But if anyone believes on the true Jesus Christ and trusts in Him alone for salvation (and not in their personal works of righteousness),[196] Jesus promises them eternal life: "Truly, truly, I say to you, he who believes has eternal life" (John 6:47). In John 17:3 Jesus also taught, "This is eternal life, that they may know Thee, the only true God, and Jesus Christ whom Thou has sent."

Jesus said that no man can serve two masters (Matthew 6:24). The practicing Mormon must choose between coming to know and serving the true Jesus Christ or continuing to serve Joseph Smith and the Mormon Church. A person cannot serve both.

Conclusion

What words of wisdom do Mormon leaders have for practicing Mormons?

In light of our discussion to this point, we think it relevant to quote some leaders in the Mormon Church and ask that practicing Mormons consider their words very carefully.

Bruce McConkie: "An antichrist is an opponent of Christ; he is one who is in opposition to the true gospel, the true church, and the true plan of salvation."[197]

Joseph Smith: "The Savior has the words of eternal life. Nothing else can profit us."[198]

Joseph Fielding Smith: "The theories of men change from day to day. Much that is taught now will tomorrow be in the discard, but the word of the Lord will endure forever."[199]

Brigham Young: "Can you destroy the decrees of the Almighty? You cannot."[200]

If objective, historical data from within the Mormon Church itself proves Mormonism a false religion, then it is tragic to remain a Mormon. Mormons who truly desire to love God have the right to know who the true God is. They have a right to know whether their own church has consistently lied to them and deceived them on vital matters.[201]

Any Mormon who wishes may examine his or her heart before God and then pray the following prayer:

> Dear God,
>
> You know that I am not only uncertain of my beliefs concerning You, but also of my spiritual condition before You. I have honestly searched my heart, and it is my desire to trust in You. By searching my heart, I have recognized I cannot earn my own salvation because, as You have said, even my best righteousness falls far short of Your holy standards.
>
> I recognize that I am a sinner worthy of Your judgment. I renounce my pride in thinking I could perfect myself and become a God. I renounce every false view of Jesus Christ and receive the true Jesus Christ as presented in the Bible. I believe that this Jesus Christ is truly God, that He effectively died for my sins on the cross and rose from the dead three days later. I believe that by receiving Him into my life I can now inherit eternal life. Right now I turn from my sins and from the false teachings of the Mormon Church. I receive the true Christ as my personal Savior. Help me to grow in the grace and knowledge of Your Son, my true Savior, Jesus Christ.

If you are a Mormon who prayed this prayer, we suggest you read the New Testament daily and attend a Christian church that honors Christ. You should tell the pastor that you are a former Mormon who has just become a Christian and ask his counsel. There are many organizations of former Mormons who are now Christians, and we suggest you contact one of them for information, counsel, and encouragement.[202]

If you have accepted Jesus as your Savior or have questions regarding doing so, contact the Ankerberg Theological Research Institute at PO Box 8977, Chattanooga, TN 37414. We'll send you material to help your spiritual growth.

Notes

1. "Tour 2: Reaching Out to the World," www.lds.org, 6/02.
2. Walter Martin, *The Maze of Mormonism* (Santa Ana, CA: Vision House, 1978), p. 21.
3. Ibid., pp. 16-21; cf. John Heinerman, Anson Shupe, *Mormon Corporate Empire* (Boston: Beacon Press, 1988).
4. Jerald Tanner and Sandra Tanner, *The Changing World of Mormonism* (Chicago, IL: Moody Press, 1981), pp. 148-70.
5. Joseph Smith, *The Pearl of Great Price* (Salt Lake City, UT: The Church of Jesus Christ of Latter-day Saints, 1967), "Writings of Joseph Smith," 2, p. 46.
6. Ibid., pp. 47-48.
7. Joseph Smith, *History of the Church of Jesus Christ of Latter-day Saints*, Vol. 1 (Salt Lake City, UT: Deseret Book Company, 1976), p. 8.
8. That the Christian denominations of Joseph Smith's time taught biblical doctrine is established by a study of the respective theological teaching of that period.
9. For example, demons routinely impersonate good angels, the spirits of the dead, and even Jesus Christ Himself. See note 191.
10. Joseph Smith, *History of the Church*, Vol. 1, p. 9.
11. For a critique, see Gordon H. Fraser, *What Does The Book of Mormon Teach? An Examination of the Historical and Scientific Statements of The Book of Mormon* (Chicago, IL: Moody Press, 1964).
12. Walter Martin, *The Kingdom of the Cults* (Minneapolis, MN: Bethany, 1970), p. 154.
13. Joseph Smith, *History of the Church*, Vol. 1, pp. 39-48, 80.
14. See *The Doctrine and Covenants of the Church of Jesus Christ of Latter-day Saints* (Salt Lake City, UT: The Church of Jesus Christ of Latter-day Saints, 1968), pp. VI-VII for a chronological listing.
15. See note 191.
16. Orson Pratt, *The Seer*, Vol. 2, No. 4, April 1854, in *The Seer* (compilation, n.p., n.d.), p. 255.
17. *Doctrine and Covenants* 1:30.
18. Pratt, *The Seer*, p. 255.
19. Bruce McConkie, *Doctrinal New Testament Commentary*, Vol. 2 (Salt Lake City, UT: Bookcraft, 1976), p. 113; cf. pp. 366, 458-59, 506-07.
20. Bruce McConkie, *Mormon Doctrine*, 2nd. ed. (Salt Lake City, UT: Bookcraft, 1977), p. 626.
21. Deseret Sunday School Union, *The Master's Church, Course A* (Salt Lake City, UT: Deseret Sunday School, Union, 1969), p. 6.
22. Harry Ropp, *The Mormon Papers: Are the Mormon Scriptures Reliable?* (Downers Grove, IL: InterVarsity, 1977), p. 119.
23. Ibid., p. 13.
24. Copy of letter from the Protestant Chapel Council, Naval Air Station Alameda, CA, to Chief of Chaplains, RADM Alvin B. Koeneman, Office

60

of the Chief of Naval Operations, Department of the Navy, Washington, DC, n.d.

25. Anthony Hoekema, *The Four Major Cults* (Grand Rapids, MI: Eerdmans, 1977), p. 30.
26. Gordon Fraser, *Is Mormonism Christian?* (Chicago, IL: Moody Press, 1977), p. 10.
27. Martin, *The Maze of Mormonism*, p. 45.
28. Tanner and Tanner, *The Changing World of Mormonism*, p. 559.
29. The bibliography in Tanner and Tanner, *The Changing World of Mormonism*, is representative.
30. Tanner and Tanner, *The Changing World of Mormonism*, pp. 192-203.
31. *Journal of Discourses*, Vol. 6 (Salt Lake City, UT: 1967, reprint of original, 1855 ed., Liverpool, England: F.D. Richards, publisher), p. 198.
32. *Elders' Journal*, Joseph Smith, ed., Vol. 1, No. 4, pp. 59-60; from Jerald Tanner and Sandra Tanner, *Mormonism—Shadow or Reality?* (Salt Lake City, UT: Utah Lighthouse Ministry, 1972), p. 3.
33. Joseph Fielding Smith, comp., *Teachings of the Prophet Joseph Smith* (Salt Lake City, UT: Deseret Book Company, 1972), p. 322.
34. Tanner and Tanner, *The Changing World of Mormonism*, pp. 398-416.
35. Joseph Smith, *History of the Church*, Vol. 1, p. LXXXVI.
36. Ibid.
37. *Journal of Discourses*, Vol. 8, p. 199.
38. Ibid., Vol. 8, p. 171.
39. Ibid., Vol. 6, p. 167.
40. Ibid., Vol. 6, p. 163; Vol. 13, p. 225.
41. *Pamphlets by Orson Pratt*, p. 38; cited in Jerald Tanner and Sandra Tanner, *The Case Against Mormonism*, Vol. 1 (Salt Lake City, UT: Utah Lighthouse Ministry, 1967), p. 6.
42. Pratt, *The Seer*, May 1854, Vol. 2, No. 5, pp. 259-60.
43. Ibid., Vol. 2, No. 3, pp. 237, 239-40.
44. Joseph Fielding Smith, *Doctrines of Salvation*, Vol. 3, comp. Bruce McConkie (Salt Lake City, UT: Bookcraft, 1976), pp. 267, 287.
45. McConkie, *Mormon Doctrine*, p. 137-38.
46. Ibid., pp. 132.
47. Ibid., passim.
48. McConkie, *Doctrinal New Testament Commentary*, Vol. 2, p. 274.
49. Ibid., Vol. 2, p. 280.
50. Ibid., Vol. 3, p. 85.
51. Ibid., Vol. 3, pp. 547, 550-51.
52. See e.g., Martin, *Kingdom of the Cults*.
53. Statement by Richard L. Evans, a member of the Council of Twelve, as cited in Leo Rosten, *Religions of America* (New York: Simon and Schuster, 1975), p. 189.
54. J.F. Smith, comp., *Teachings of the Prophet*, p. 370.
55. McConkie, *Mormon Doctrine*, p. 317.
56. Ibid., pp. 576-77.
57. J.F. Smith, *Teachings of the Prophet*, p. 347; Duane S. Crowther, *Life Everlasting* (Salt Lake City, UT: Bookcraft, 1988), pp. 360-61.
58. McConkie, *Doctrinal New Testament Commentary*, Vol. 2, p. 78.
59. Joseph Smith, *History of the Church*, Vol. 6, p. 305.
60. J.F. Smith, *Teaching of the Prophet*, pp. 345-46.
61. Ibid., p. 371.
62. Ibid., p. 181.
63. McConkie, *Mormon Doctrine*, p. 250.
64. McConkie, *Doctrinal New Testament Commentary*, Vol. 2, p. 160.
65. *Journal of Discourses*, Vol. 13, p. 308.
66. Pratt, *The Seer*, November, 1853, Vol. 1, No. 11, p. 172.
67. Crowther, *Life Everlasting*, p. 340.
68. *Journal of Discourses*, Vol. 3, p. 93.
69. Milton R. Hunter, *The Gospel Through the Ages* (Salt Lake City, UT: Deseret Books, 1958), pp. 104, 114-15, cited in Tanner and Tanner, *The Changing World of Mormonism*, p. 177.
70. *Salt Lake Tribune*, Oct. 6, 1974, p. 1, from Tanner and Tanner, *The Changing World of Mormonism*, p. 188.

71. Gordon Hinckley, as quoted under "Basic Beliefs," "Frequently Asked Questions," "Theology" at www.lds.org, July 2002.
72. Taken from www.lds.org, July 2002.
73. James Talmage, *A Study of the Articles of Faith* (Salt Lake City, UT: The Church of Jesus Christ of Latter-day Saints, 1974), p. 471.
74. J.H. Evans, *An American Prophet* (1933), p. 241, cited in Hoekema, *The Four Major Cults*, p. 54.
75. McConkie, *Doctrinal New Testament Commentary*, Vol. 3, p. 238.
76. McConkie, *Mormon Doctrine*, p. 129.
77. Ibid., p. 257.
78. Milton Hunter, *The Gospel Through the Ages* (1958), p. 21, from Tanner and Tanner, *The Changing World of Mormonism*, p. 519.
79. McConkie, *Mormon Doctrine*, p. 169; cf. J.F. Smith, *Doctrines of Salvation*, Vol. 1, p. 75.
80. J.F. Smith, *Doctrines of Salvation*, Vol. 1, p. 18.
81. Carlfred B. Broderick, in *Dialogue: A Journal of Mormon Thought*, Autumn, 1967, pp. 100-01, from Tanner and Tanner, *The Changing World of Mormonism*, p. 180.
82. J.F. Smith, *Doctrines of Salvation*, Vol. 1, p. 18.
83. McConkie, *Mormon Doctrine*, p. 547.
84. Brigham Young in *Deseret News*, October 10, 1866, from Tanner and Tanner, *The Changing World of Mormonism*, p. 180.
85. Pratt, *The Seer*, November 1853, Vol. 1, No. 11, p. 172.
86. James Talmage, *Jesus the Christ* (Salt Lake City, UT: Deseret Book Company, 1976), p. 31.
87. McConkie, *Mormon Doctrine*, p. 116.
88. McConkie, *Mormon Doctrine*, pp. 176-77, 234, 670; McConkie, *Doctrinal New Testament Commentary*, Vol. 3, pp. 284-85.
89. Talmage, *Articles of Faith*, p. 107.
90. J.F. Smith, *Doctrines of Salvation*, Vol. 2, p. 139.
91. McConkie, *Doctrinal New Testament Commentary*, Vol. 2, p. 229.
92. E.g., The Book of Mormon: 2 Nephi 25:23; Alma 7:16; Mosiah 5:7,8; 13:27,28; 2 Nephi 9:23,24; *Doctrine and Covenants*, 7:37; 132:12.
93. *Journal of Discourses*, Vol. 3, p. 269.
94. Talmage, *Jesus the Christ*, p. 5.
95. Joseph Fielding Smith, *The Way to Perfection* (Salt Lake City, UT: Deseret Book Company, 1975), p. 189.
96. McConkie, *Doctrinal New Testament Commentary*, Vol. 2, p. 294, cf. p. 279.
97. McConkie, *Mormon Doctrine*, p. 61.
98. The Book of Mormon: Helaman 14:15-16; 2 Nephi 2:26.
99. Crowther, *Life Everlasting*, p. 233; *What the Mormons Think of...Christ*, p. 28.
100. E.g., *The Master's Church, Course A*, p. 96; McConkie, *Doctrinal New Testament Commentary*, Vol. 2, pp. 242-43; Talmage, *Articles of Faith*, pp. 87-89.
101. *What the Mormons Think of...Christ*, pp. 27-28.
102. *Journal of Discourses*, Vol. 4, p. 220.
103. Tanner and Tanner, *The Changing World of Mormonism*, pp. 490-504; cf. John Ahmanson, *Secret History: An Eye Witness Account of the Rise of Mormonism* (Chicago, IL: Moody Press, 1984); Stephen Naifeh and Gregory White Smith, *The Mormon Murders: A True Story of Greed, Forgery, Deceit and Death* (New York, NY: Weidenfeld and Nicholson, 1988).
104. *Journal of Discourses*, Vol. 21, p. 81.
105. Cf. Tanner and Tanner, *The Changing World of Mormonism*; Martin, *The Maze of Mormonism*, etc.
106. *Journal of Discourses*, Vol. 14, p. 216.
107. *The Master's Church, Course A*, p. 225.
108. McConkie, *Doctrinal New Testament Commentary*, Vol. 2, p. 274; Joseph Smith, *History of the Church*, Vol. 1, p. XCI.
109. F.F. Bruce, *The New Testament Documents: Are They Reliable?* (Downers Grove, IL: InterVarsity Press, 1969); Norman L. Geisler, William E. Nix, *A General Introduction to the Bible*, rev. ed. (Chicago, IL: Moody, 1986).

110. At the time of his "first vision," 1820, Joseph Smith Jr. was 15 according to his statement recorded in *The Pearl of Great Price*.

111. *Dialogue: A Journal of Mormon Thought*, Autumn 1966, p. 29; David L. McKay, *Gospel Ideals*, p. 85; John A. Widtsow, *Joseph Smith, Seeker After Truth*, p. 19; Paul Cheesman, "An Analysis of the Accounts Relating Joseph Smith's Early Visions," BYU graduate thesis, May 1975, p. 75, cited in Tanner and Tanner, *The Changing World of Mormonism*, p. 151; Jerald Tanner and Sandra Tanner, *Joseph Smith's Strange Account of the First Vision* (Salt Lake City, UT: Utah Lighthouse Ministry, n.d.), p. 1; Tanner and Tanner, *Mormonism: Shadow or Reality?* p. 143; Martin, *The Maze of Mormonism*, pp. 26-30, cf. Tanner and Tanner, *The Changing World of Mormonism*, Chapter 6.

112. Tanner and Tanner, *The Changing World of Mormonism*, p. 148.

113. Ibid., pp. 10, 149-55.

114. Wesley P. Walters, *New Light on Mormon Origins from the Palmyra [New York] Revival* (n.p., 1967), cf. Tanner and Tanner, *The Changing World of Mormonism*, pp. 166-71 and Marvin W. Cowan, *Mormon Claims Answered* (Salt Lake City, UT: Marvin W. Cowan), pp. 1-10.

115. Tanner and Tanner, *The Changing World of Mormonism*, pp. 155-56.

116. Ibid., p. 156.

117. Ibid., pp. 148-71.

118. Hugh Nibley, *An Approach to The Book of Mormon* (1957), p. 13, cited in Tanner and Tanner, *The Case Against Mormonism*, Vol. 2, p. 63.

119. Joseph Fielding Smith, *Answers to Gospel Questions*, Vol. 2 (Salt Lake City, UT: Deseret Book Company, 1976), p. 199.

120. E.g., Jerald Tanner and Sandra Tanner, *Joseph Smith and Money Digging* (Salt Lake City, UT: Utah Lighthouse Ministry, 1970).

121. *The Saints' Herald*, May 19, 1888, p. 310, from Tanner and Tanner, *The Changing World of Mormonism*, p. 81.

122. Fawn Brodie, *No Man Knows My History: The Life of Joseph Smith* (New York, NY: Alfred A. Knopf, rev. 1976), p. 69.

123. Ibid., pp. 69-70, citing *Millennial Harbinger*, Vol. 2, February 18, 1931, p. 85.

124. B.H. Roberts, *Studies of The Book of Mormon*, available from Utah Lighthouse Ministry, Box 1884, Salt Lake City, UT 84110.

125. See e.g., Hal Hougey, *A Parallel—The Basis of The Book of Mormon: B.H. Roberts "Parallel" of The Book of Mormon to View of the Hebrews* (Concord, CA: Pacific Publishing Company, 1963), p. 4; Ropp, *The Mormon Papers*, p. 36; cf. Ethan Smith, *View of the Hebrews*, available from Utah Lighthouse Ministry, Box 1884, Salt Lake City, UT 84110.

126. Hoekema, *The Four Major Cults*, p. 85.

127. Tanner and Tanner, *The Case Against Mormonism*, Vol. 2, pp. 87-102.

128. Fraser, *Is Mormonism Christian?* p. 143; cf. p. 145.

129. This letter and many others like it are reproduced in Jerry and Marian Bodine, *Whom Can You Trust?* (Santa Ana, CA: Christ for the Cults, 1979), p. 16.

130. Ibid., p. 3, citing letter of Frank Roberts, Jr., director, to Mr. Marvin Cowan, January 24, 1963.

131. Ibid., p. 13, citing letter of Mr. Hermansen to Mr. Gregory R. Shannon, May 29, 1978.

132. See Sir William Ramsay, *The Bearing of Recent Discovery on the Trustworthiness of the New Testament* (Grand Rapids, MI: Baker Book House, 1979, reprint); Tanner and Tanner, *The Changing World of Mormonism*, pp. 140-41; cf. Jerald Tanner and Sandra Tanner, *Archeology and The Book of Mormon*, available from Utah Lighthouse Ministry, Box 1884, Salt Lake City, UT 84110.

133. Martin, *The Maze of Mormonism*, pp. 68-9; cf. Gordon H. Fraser, *Joseph and the Golden Plates: A Close Look at The Book of Mormon* (Eugene, OR: Gordon H. Fraser Publisher, 1978).

134. According to eyewitness accounts by Emma Smith, Martin Harris, and David Whitmer, Joseph Smith Jr. would put a seer stone into a hat, put his face in the hat, drawing it close to shut out light. Individual words or letters would appear, and Joseph would speak them out loud to a scribe.

If a mistake was made, the image Joseph saw would remain until the scribe corrected it. See "The Testimony of the Three Witnesses" in the front of The Book of Mormon.

135. See Ropp, *The Mormon Papers*, ch. 4, Appendix C; Tanner and Tanner, *The Changing World of Mormonism*, pp. 38-63; *Joseph Smith Begins His Work*, Vol. 2 (photo reprint of the 1833 *Book of Commandments* and the 1835 *Doctrine and Covenants*), available from Utah Lighthouse Ministry, Box 1884, Salt Lake City, UT 84110.

136. E.g., J.F. Smith, *Doctrines of Salvation*, Vol. 1, p. 170; and Tanner and Tanner, *The Changing World of Mormonism*, p. 39.

137. Available from Utah Lighthouse Ministry, Box 1884, Salt Lake City, UT 84110.

138. Ibid.

139. Tanner and Tanner, *The Changing World of Mormonism*, pp. 329-63.

140. See the following titles available from Utah Lighthouse Ministry, Box 1884, Salt Lake City, UT 84110: Wesley Walters, *Joseph Smith Among the Egyptians*; H. Michael Marquardt, *The Book of Abraham Papyrus Found*; *Joseph Smith's Egyptian Alphabet and Grammar*; and F.S. Spaulding, *Why Egyptologists Reject The Book of Abraham*.

141. See the materials from Tanner and Tanner, Utah Lighthouse Ministry, Box 1884, Salt Lake City, UT 84110.

142. Martin, *Kingdom of the Cults*, p. 181.

143. See e.g., Tanner and Tanner, *The Changing World of Mormonism*, pp. 29-66; see also Jerald and Sandra Tanner, *Falsification of Joseph Smith's History*; D. Michael Quinn, "On Being a Mormon Historian," available from Utah Lighthouse Ministry, Box 1884, Salt Lake City, UT 84110; Tanner and Tanner, *Mormon Spies, Hughes and the CIA* (Salt Lake City, UT: Utah Lighthouse Ministry).

144. Tanner and Tanner, *The Changing World of Mormonism*.

145. *The Evening and Morning Star*, July 1833, p. 1.

146. McConkie, *Doctrinal New Testament Commentary*, Vol. 1, p. 252.

147. Talmage, *Articles of Faith*, pp. 7-8.

148. *Journal of Discourses*, Vol. 10, p. 344.

149. *Journal of Discourses*, Vol. 13, p. 362.

150. Clause J. Hansen, *Dialogue: A Journal of Mormon Thought*, Autumn 1966, p. 74.

151. J.F. Smith, *The Way to Perfection* (1935 ed.), p. 270.

152. Ropp, *The Mormon Papers*, p. 64; cf. "Rebellion in South Carolina," *Evening and Morning Star*, February 1833.

153. Tanner and Tanner, *The Changing World of Mormonism*, pp. 428-30.

154. Ibid., pp. 417-30.

155. *Mormonia: A Quarterly Bibliography of Works on Mormonism*, Fall 1972, p. 89. Published in 1972-73, *Mormonia* editions are available at Brigham Young University library and elsewhere.

156. *Salt Lake Tribune*, October 7, 1972, pp. 22-3 cited in Tanner and Tanner, *Mormonism Like Watergate? An Answer to Hugh Nibley*, 1974, p. 4.

157. Foreword in Tanner and Tanner, *The Changing World of Mormonism*, p. 11.

158. Talmage, *Articles of Faith*, p. 296.

159. Ibid., p. 311.

160. Ibid.

161. E.g., *Journal of Discourses*, Vol. 2, p. 338; Vol. 3, pp. 155-57.

162. *Doctrine and Covenants* 93:1; 67:10-14; McConkie, *Mormon Doctrine*, p. 664; *Journal of Discourses*, Vol. 1, pp. 13-15; Vol. 2, pp. 44-6; see Question 23.

163. McConkie, *Mormon Doctrine*, p. 650, citing *Doctrine and Covenants* 102:2,9,23; 107:39; 128:11.

164. McConkie, *Mormon Doctrine*, p. 645.

165. E.g., *Journal of Discourses*, Vol. 16, p. 46; The Book of Mormon, Moroni 10:4-5.

166. Martin, *The Maze of Mormonism*, p. 220; cf. J.F. Smith, *The Way to Perfection*, pp. 318-19; McConkie, *Doctrinal New Testament Commentary*, pp. 225-26; McConkie, *Mormon Doctrine*, pp. 35-36, 762.

167. Available from Utah Lighthouse Ministry, Box 1884, Salt Lake City, UT 84110.
168. Martin, *The Maze of Mormonism*, p. 211.
169. Tanner and Tanner, *The Changing World of Mormonism*, p. 10; Einar Anderson, *Inside Story of Mormonism* (Grand Rapids, MI: Kregel, 1974), p. 22.
170. Kurt Koch, *Christian Counseling and Occultism* (Grand Rapids, MI: Kregel 1972), pp. 184-87.
171. *Deseret News*, May 29, 1852; cf. Tanner and Tanner, *The Changing World of Mormonism*, p. 159.
172. E.g., Tanner and Tanner, *The Changing World of Mormonism*, pp. 77-85.
173. Ibid., pp. 67-69.
174. Ibid., pp. 88-91; cf. Jack Adamson and Reed Durham, Jr., *No Help for the Widow's Son: Mormonism and Masonry* (Nauvoo, IL: Martin Publishing Company, 1980), pp. 32-33.
175. Tanner and Tanner, *The Changing World of Mormonism*, pp. 67-80.
176. Ibid., pp. 80-84; cf. Tanner and Tanner, *Joseph Smith and Money Digging*, p. 7.
177. Tanner and Tanner, *Joseph Smith and Money Digging*, pp. 11-13.
178. Martin, *The Maze of Mormonism*, p. 218; see Question 23.
179. J.F. Smith, *Teachings of the Prophet*, pp. 326, 243, 338, 363.
180. *Journal of Discourses*, Vol. 6, p. 349; cf. J.F. Smith, *Teachings of the Prophet*, pp. 222-23, 180, 191-93, 363.
181. Joseph Smith, *Improvement Era*, Vol. 39, April 1936, p. 200; *Times and Seasons*, Vol. 2, p. 546, cited in Joseph Heinerman, *Spirit World Manifestations: Accounts of Divine Aid in Genealogical and Temple and Other Assistance to Latter-day Saints* (Salt Lake City, UT: Joseph Lyon and Associates, 1986).
182. Heinerman, *Spirit World Manifestations*, p. 29.
183. McConkie, *Doctrinal New Testament Commentary*, Vol. 3, pp. 140-41; LeGrand Richards, *A Marvelous Work and a Wonder* (Salt Lake City, UT: Deseret Book Company, 1975), p. 426.
184. E.g., J.F. Smith, *Answers to Gospel Questions*, Vol. 1, p. 47; Joseph Smith, *History of the Church*, Vol. 2, p. 380; Vol. 4, p. 231.
185. Parley P. Pratt, "Spiritual Communication," *Journal of Discourses*, Vol. 2, pp. 44-45.
186. Charles Penrose, *Mormon Doctrine* (1888), pp. 40-41, cited in Martin, *The Maze of Mormonism*, p. 225.
187. J.F. Smith, *Gospel Doctrine*, pp. 436-37.
188. E.g., *Journal of Discourses*, Vol. 3, p. 369; Vol. 7, p. 240; Crowther, *Life Everlasting*, p. 60; *Deseret Weekly News*, Vol. 53, p. 112.
189. *Journal of Discourses*, Vol. 7, p. 240.
190. John A. Widtsoe, *Discourses of Brigham Young* (Salt Lake City, UT: Deseret Book Company, 1976), pp. 378-80, citing *Journal of Discourses*, Vol. 7, p. 332; Vol. 6, p. 349.
191. John Ankerberg and John Weldon, *The Facts on Spirit Guides* (Eugene, OR: Harvest House, 1988) and *The Facts on the Occult* (Eugene, OR: Harvest House, 1991); Merrill Unger, *Biblical Demonology* (Wheaton, IL: Scripture Press, 1971); Raphael Gasson, *The Challenging Counterfeit* (Plainfield, NJ: Logos, 1971).
192. Ibid.
193. Joseph Heinerman, *Eternal Testimonies: Inspired Testimonies of Latter-day Saints* (Salt Lake City, UT: Magazine Printing and Publishing, 1982).
194. Heinerman, *Spirit World Manifestations*, pp. 7, 277, 280.
195. Crowther, *Life Everlasting*, p. 151.
196. Floyd McElveen, *Will the Saints Go Marching In?* (Glendale, CA: Regal, 1977), p. 168.
197. McConkie, *Mormon Doctrine*, p. 39.
198. J.F. Smith, *Teachings of the Prophet*, p. 364.
199. J.F. Smith, *Doctrines of Salvation*, Vol. 1., p. 324.
200. *Journal of Discourses*, Vol. 10., p. 250.
201. See note 141.
202. See note 137.